I'm Expecting

I0191160

I'm Expecting

BIRTHING THE

PROMISES
OF God

A.R. SMITH

Get
WRITE
PUBLISHING

I'm Expecting: Birthing the Promises of God

Copyright © 2017 by A.R. Smith

All rights reserved. No part of this publication may be reproduced, distributed, or transmitted in any form or by any means, including photocopying, recording, or other electronic or mechanical methods, without the prior written permission of the publisher, except in the case of brief quotations embodied in critical reviews and certain other noncommercial uses permitted by copyright law.

Except where noted, all Scriptures are taken from the King James Bible version.

Printed in the United States of America.

ISBN: 978-1-945456-55-8

Cover Design:
Alex Cotton - Ginisis Media Group

Editing:
Get Write Publishing

I dedicate this book to my mother, sisters, husband, and children. You all have inspired me to be great in your own unique way.

I also dedicate this book to every warrior who will come in contact with this book. This is your season to birth the promises of God without apology or restraint.

ACKNOWLEDGEMENTS

I express my deepest gratitude to those who've played a key role in the success of this book.

To all those who have prayed, supported, donated, proofread, formatted and edited, I am truly grateful for your contribution.

I would like to thank my husband Charles my family and our church family for your support and encouragement while I was on this road to authorship.

Last but not least, I would like to thank my Pastors Apostle Paul and Lady Yolonda Kelker for believing in me and teaching me to not give up on my dreams.

There are so many who've made an impact on my life that haven't been named but you know who you are. I sincerely thank you from my heart.

Gratefully Written,

Ambassador A.R. Smith

TABLE OF CONTENTS

Introduction

103   Special Prayer

INTRODUCTION

I greet you in the name of our Lord and Savior! I am so excited to be embarking on this journey with you while birthing the promises of God. First, I would like to commend you for choosing to make a change in your life today! You have made a conscious decision to move forward in fulfilling the things of God. You have identified that there is greatness within you and it's ready to spring forth as a river of success and prosperity.

You know without a shadow of a doubt that God has given you purpose and a vision that will contribute to the Kingdom of God. He has gifted you with many witty inventions and ideas, but the question you're asking yourself is, "How? When, will I see the manifestation of my purpose and vision?" I asked God the same question and the response God gave me was, "I'm going to give it to you. The how belongs to you, and the when belongs to Me (God)!" I didn't understand it at first, but now I have a greater understanding of that revelation.

The "how" is considered the way something is accomplished or carried out and the "when" is the perfect (divine) timing of God. When we don't see the manifestation of the promise, we get discouraged and ultimately become stuck or stagnant.

We live in a society where we have developed a microwave mentality. We want everything quick, fast, and in a hurry. Unfortunately, God does not operate off our microwave system. Booker T. Washington said it best: Nothing ever comes to one, that is worth having, except as a result of hard work. There is some plowing and sowing that must take place before we reap a Kingdom reward.

This book is designed by God to assist you in excelling during your spiritual birthing process. It will teach you how to overcome the wiles, the tactics and the plots of the enemy. I declare that by the end of this book, your baby (promise) will no longer be stuck! You will have the proper fundamentals to help assist with pushing and birthing the promises of God.

From this day forward, you will seize your destiny, grasp your purpose and capture opportunities. Watch God fulfill the promises in your life. I declare that this is a good day to declare a new day and walk in a new way in life. Congratulations, you are expecting!

CHAPTER 1

The Foundation

Have you ever heard the phrase, "You can't see the forest for the trees?" This saying applies to a person who puts too much emphasis on small things and fails to understand the plans and principles of life on a larger scale. The truth is that some people live this phrase every day of their lives.

It's hard for people to comprehend Canaan when they feel they only have Egypt as an option. Canaan represents a land of promise and a state of liberation and freedom. Egypt represents oppression and a place of enslavement and bondage. People have allowed the enemy to tell them that there is no way out of Egypt! Your mama didn't get out, her mama or daddy didn't get out, so what makes you think you're getting out? As the saints of old used to say, "Satan you're a liar and a defeated foe!"

When God reveals to you the blessings He has prepared for you (whether by dream or vision), anything that opposes the truth or is contrary to that revelation is not of God. If you choose to believe the contrary, you are forfeiting the blessing in exchange for the illusion that has been presented to you.

I have been guilty of believing the illusion in the past, but through studying the Word of God, His wisdom and understanding has increased within me. I have learned to walk by faith and not by sight. I learned that I just can't quote the Bible, but I too have to be a doer of the Word.

Hebrews 11:1-3

1 **Now faith is the substance of things hoped for, the evidence of things not seen.**

2 **For by it the elders obtained a good report.**

3 **Through faith we understand that the worlds were framed by the word of God, so that things which are seen were not made of things which do appear.**

Now- At the present time or moment; without further delay; immediately; at once.

Faith- The conviction that God exists and is the creator and ruler of all things, the provider and bestower of eternal salvation through Christ; A strong and welcome conviction or belief that Jesus is the messiah through whom we obtain eternal salvation in the kingdom of God

Substance- A substructure or foundation; confidence, firm trust, and assurance.

Thing- A matter of concern, whatever may be possessed or owned or be the object of a right, a product of work or activity.

Hope- To wait for salvation with joy and full confidence; to trust in

(Strong's Concordance)

I chose this scripture because it's widely known among Christianity today. Most people don't know what this scripture signifies or represents, but because we know it and quote it; many have adjusted the scripture to conform to their situation.

Personally, I used to think it's pretty much self-explanatory. I found out very quickly that this wasn't the truth. Holy Spirit has taught me that faith is much more than my bills being paid or my financial status; those things can change at any time. Faith cannot and will not change since it is connected to God and Jesus Christ.

When we put our faith in action, we are proclaiming before the heavens that we believe that God is the Supreme Authority Who sent Authority (Jesus) to leave us Authority (Holy Spirit) to teach us Authority and move in Authority. Yes, you have faith to move mountains and they shall obey. Yes, you have faith to look at the forest: the larger plan, the immeasurable amount of favor, and monumental promises. Glory to God!

This foundation was written to shed light on the chapters in this book. There will be many days you won't feel prosperous. Your bank account may not be showing prosperity; however, you have to rest in assurance and know that change has come.

This is the day that heaven has invaded your ear(th) to provoke you to listen to what God has in store for you. This process will teach you what must be done and what is expected during the birthing stages. As the author, I want you to understand that I can identify with you, so when you see the word "we," I'm talking to the both of us. When you see the word "you," it is meant to empower and awaken your creativity, witty inventions and ideas so that you may have much success in the body of Christ.

CHAPTER 2

Invitation to Salvation

Salv(e)- a balm used to promote healing of the skin or as protection.

ation- the action or process of doing something

"Eye salve was used in the Bible days to restore natural vision. Salvation is given to restore insight to the spiritually blind." – A.R. Smith

It is my heart's desire for everyone that comes in contact with this book to receive a clear and precise understanding of salvation, because no one can possess the promises of God without it. As the author, I don't want to assume that the reader is saved just because they are reading this book. I wouldn't want the reader to miss out on an opportunity of salvation. If you are already saved, this chapter will be a reminder of how blessed we are to be engrafted into the Kingdom of God.

There are many facets that could be covered about salvation, but I will give the basic overview of the topic. It's not my intent to offend or judge; however, I am required as an ambassador of the gospel to express through writing the truth so that you can be made free. Truth is, we live in a society where people create their own perception of what salvation is to fit their own personal needs or situations.

The term salvation has been used so loosely that people don't grasp the understanding and the power of the word. It's more than just going down to the altar on Sunday morning, raising your hand, and confessing that Jesus is Lord.

The altar is a place of surrender. It is an outward declaration and commitment that a person makes before heaven and earth. A person makes the decision to offer themselves as a living sacrifice and accept the internal working of God. This conversion is intertwined with a spiritual deliverance from sin, death, and the works of darkness.

Salvation is a gift that is extended to everyone on God's green earth, yet some will not accept it because it will require them to surrender some things that are very dear to them. Some believe they will miss out on happiness and fun, or that it will affect relationships with family members or friends. Some people simply believe they have time to accept salvation with words like, "I'm not going to die right now," or "I'm in good health and I do good deeds." In reality, when it comes to where you'll spend your eternity, the issue is extremely time-sensitive.

Don't put off for tomorrow what can be done today. We may delay, but time is continuously going. Every second in your day is an opportunity to accept the gift of salvation.

Let me dispel this myth: being saved is not boring, depressing, or sad at all! I personally apologize to you on the behalf of those who didn't exemplify that being saved is absolutely the most amazing milestone that could ever take place in your lifetime!

Don't be afraid to surrender to God. He's not trying to change the essence of who you are, He's just enhancing who you are in Christ. You are simply surrendering your desires to take on His desires and follow after His ways and likeness.

When Jesus called the first disciples, they were willing to give up everything to follow him.

Matthew 4:18-22

18 And Jesus, walking by the sea of Galilee, saw two brethren, Simon called Peter, and Andrew his brother, casting a net into the sea: for they were fishers.

19 And he saith unto them, Follow me, and I will make you fishers of men.

20 And they straightway left their nets, and followed him.

21 And going on from thence, he saw other two brethren, James the son of Zebedee, and John his brother, in a ship with Zebedee their father, mending their nets; and he called them.

22 And they immediately left the ship and their father, and followed him.

In those days, if a Rabbi considered you to be a teachable student, they would say "follow me." This would insinuate that the individual has potential to be just like him, emulate him and would submit to the rabbi's authoritative teachings. Follow me also means to come and be with me. The disciples knew they were receiving the opportunity of a lifetime.

Not everyone had the privilege to hear the words "follow me," even though they desired it. In the text, we see that the invitation to follow Jesus was immediately accepted. Why?

They understood the magnitude of the invitation.

In the same way that Jesus chose the first disciples; through the power of the crucifixion, death, burial, and resurrection, He has chosen you! He desires for you to be just like Him, to listen to Him, to emulate Him, and to submit to His authoritative teachings.

Jesus paid the cost for us on Calvary so that we could receive a new identity, in addition to eternal life. By Jesus paying the price for us, we are freely given access to heaven's possessions.

Cost- *A payment that has to be required, before it can be acquired or done; an amount that has to be paid or spent to buy or obtain something.*

Give- *To pay or transfer possession to another in exchange for something; to grant; to impart.*

Romans 6:23
For the wages of sin *is* death; but the gift of God *is* eternal life through Jesus Christ our Lord.

The blood of Jesus that was shed for me and you, is still covering our sins today! It will make you free, detach you from death and loose you from satan's kingdom.

9

Once Saved, Always Saved

In Christiandom, there is a saying, "Once saved, always saved." I too went along with this phrase. It encourages people to adopt the kind of thinking that would allow them to say something like, "I can do what I want on Friday and Saturday as long as I get up and go to church on Sunday morning. I'm alright. After all, God's still working on me" (insert sarcasm).

When God opened the eyes of my under-standing, I realized that this was a lie uttered and provoked by the traditions of man. This line of thinking is not representative of our Heavenly Father. Now, most people won't agree with this because the Scripture says:

Romans 10:13
For whosoever shall call upon the name of the Lord shall be saved.

This scripture is not implying that if you say the word Lord that you are saved. Many people skip over the requirements of the prior scripture in Romans Chapter 10:

Romans 10:9-13

9 That if thou shalt confess with thy mouth the Lord Jesus, and shalt believe in thine heart that God hath raised him from the dead, thou shalt be saved.

10 For with the heart man believeth unto righteousness; and with the mouth confession is made unto salvation.

11 For the scripture saith, Whosoever believeth on him shall not be ashamed.

12 For there is no difference between the Jew and the Greek: for the same Lord over all is rich unto all that call upon him.

13 For whosoever shall call upon the name of the Lord shall be saved.

Matthew 7:21

Not every one that saith to me 'Lord, Lord' will enter into the kingdom of heaven; but he that doeth the will of my Father which is in heaven.

In order to be in a position to call upon the name of the Lord, you have to accept Jesus in your life as your Lord and Savior. This is not a one-time declaration. Understand that there is maintenance to salvation. For example, when a person buys a new car, they will find a manual in the glove department. The manual gives the owner instructions on how to operate the vehicle as well as what has to be maintained in order for the car to perform at its highest potential. If the owner fails to follow the instructions, there is a possibility that the engine could lock up due to low oil or the car could lose power because of an old battery. If these issues are not corrected, the car is inoperable until the power is restored back to the vehicle.

There is no difference spiritually. We have the Bible that gives us instructions of what we must do in order to maintain our salvation and perform at our highest potential. Question: If salvation doesn't need to be maintained, why is hell prevalent? What is the purpose of the perfect plan of salvation if the whole world is going to heaven? There you have—it once saved is not always saved!

Now, I'm not saying that you won't struggle with different conditions or circumstances; that's expected when you are a new believer or convert to the kingdom of God. If you've been saved for three or more years or are a seasoned Christian of the gospel of Christ, some struggles shouldn't come so easy. We have overcome by the blood of the Lamb.

See, salvation wasn't extended to us so that we could remain the same person we were previously. Jesus willingly laid down His life because He knew that our sins separated us from the Father. Jesus stood in the gap for us and reconciled a righteous God with an unrighteous people. By doing so, we are no longer under condemnation. Glory to God!

John 3:16-18
16 For God so loved the world, that he gave his only begotten son, that whosoever believeth in him should not perish but have everlasting life.
17 For God sent not his Son into the world to condemn the world; but that the world through him might be saved.
18 He that believeth on him is not condemned: but he that believeth not is condemned already, because he hath not believed in the name of the only begotten Son of God.

The Sacrifice

The Old Testament describes the different types of sacrifices that consisted of grain and animal offerings. The sacrifices were offered unto the Lord for various reasons, but I want to focus on the animal sacrifice. The blood of the animal sacrifice is significant because it symbolized:

- Forgiveness
- Atonement
- A temporary covering for sin
- Life

Leviticus 17:11

For the life of the flesh is in the blood: and I have given it to you upon the altar to make an atonement for your souls: for it is the blood that maketh an atonement for the soul.

Jesus, who is the Lamb of God, became the ultimate sacrifice for our sins. This was no longer a temporary remedy, but became a permanent covering! His blood has cleansed, redeemed and delivered us from the evil one. The blood of Jesus is powerful and it empowers us to move in righteousness and truth.

The saints of old used to sing a song with the words, *"Power, power, wonder-working power in the blood..."* Imagine, if we didn't have blood in our natural bodies; there would be no life in us! The same is true for the body of Christ.

Without the blood, there would be no life in us. It is the blood that brings nourishment and oxygen to the body. The blood also pushes toxins out the body. This gives a new meaning to being blood-bought!

Lovest Thou Me?

What does the word **love** mean to you? Sometimes we use the word to describe a plethora of things; however, love can be expressed in different aspects. Let's look at the definitions below:

Phileo- A natural affection shown to friends or family members, or to have interest in something or someone. It also could be considered as a soulish response "I love my spouse" "I love the color red" or "I love ice cream."

Agape- The actions of John 3:16, it's sacrificial; it's obedient, and committed. It's not tied to the soul but it's tied to the will of God.

John 21:15–19 is the perfect example of phileo and agape love.

John 21:15-19

15 So when they had dined, Jesus saith to Simon Peter, Simon, son of Jonas, lovest thou me more than these? He saith unto him, Yea, Lord; thou knowest that I love thee. He saith unto him, Feed my lambs.

16 He saith to him again the second time, Simon, son of Jonas, lovest thou me? He saith unto him, Yea, Lord; thou knowest that I love thee. He saith unto him, Feed my sheep.

17 He saith unto him the third time, Simon, son of Jonas, lovest thou me? Peter was grieved because he said unto him the third time, Lovest thou me? And he said unto him, Lord, thou knowest all things; thou knowest that I love thee. Jesus saith unto him, Feed my sheep.

18 Verily, verily, I say unto thee, When thou wast young, thou girdest thyself, and walkedst whither thou wouldest: but when thou shalt be old, thou shalt stretch forth thy hands, and another shall gird thee, and carry thee whither thou wouldest not.

19 This spake he, signifying by what death he should glorify God. And when he had spoken this, he saith unto him, Follow me.

Here Jesus is asking Peter does he agape (love) him, but Peter kept responding in phileo (love).

In other words, Jesus wanted to know if Peter loved Him with the love of God. When Jesus said "feed my lamb, or feed my sheep," He was asking Peter if he was willing to be a living sacrifice for His sake. Was Peter willing to serve and carry out the assignment? Beforehand, Peter denied Jesus three times and yet Jesus extended agape love.

See, salvation is love that is extended to the undeserved. Are you willing to extend agape love to people who deny you or wrongfully accuse you? Or to those who spitefully use you? Are you willing to love both your enemy and your neighbor in the same way that you love yourself? I heard someone say, "It's easy to love those who love you, but can you love those who hate you?" The same people who spit on Him and crucified Him—He loved them too!

Sanctification

Baker's Evangelical Dictionary states that: The generic meaning of sanctification is "the state of proper functioning." To sanctify someone or something is to set that person or thing apart for the use intended by its designer.

Sanctification and holiness are interchangeable. Contrary to popular belief, you can be holy. For so long, people looked at holiness as an unachievable position; however, it can be obtained. Truth is, you can't have genuine salvation without being sanctified/holy.

The natural mind perceives holiness as wearing long skirts down to your knees or ankles, not showing your arms, or not wearing red lipstick, yet this is the spirit of religion. The spirit of religion presents an outward appearance of holiness, though inward transformation hasn't taken place.

The Bible says this is considered as having a form of godliness and denying the power thereof. Don't just look holy, be holy. Father wouldn't tell us to be holy if it couldn't be obtained.

1 Peter 1:13-16
13 Wherefore gird up the loins of your mind, be sober, and hope to the end for

the grace that is to be brought unto you at the revelation of Jesus Christ;

14 **As obedient children, not fashioning yourselves according to the former lusts in your ignorance:**

15 **But as he which hath called you is holy, so be ye holy in all manner of conversation;**

16 **Because it is written, Be ye holy; for I am holy.**

First, you received salvation. Sanctification cleansed you from all the worldly influences and filthiness, now holiness has been produced. Father gives us instructions to maintain this spiritual state of mind.

Be sober- Having a sober mind; a spiritual clear conscience and an alertness of your surroundings. Not being influenced by the kingdom of darkness.

Obedient- To hear God's Word and act accordingly; obey; obedience is connected to trust and faith.

Do not Fashion or pattern yourself after the world- Do not take on the former image of

Satan or the behavior; or the evil desires prior to salvation.

There is a spiritual working that God will do in us but it's according to the individual's will. God has brought us out of darkness into His marvelous light, but He has given us the power to maintain the victory. When we apply the instructions to our lives, then we are entitled to the promises that are released through obedience.

In the chapters to come we will talk about the promises of God, but the most important thing is to make sure that you are in a position to receive them. Know that you have genuine salvation, and that you have been sanctified by the blood of the Lamb so you can walk in holiness wholly and completely.

There will be days you may fall or you may speak things in the atmosphere that don't speak to your destiny. Get up, dust yourself off, repent wholeheartedly and remember Romans 8:1 *"There is therefore now no condemnation to them which are in Christ Jesus who walk not after the flesh, but after the spirit. Old things have passed away, behold all things made new!"* Glory to God. If you agree with the truth confess this prayer with me. If you are a reader, and haven't accepted Jesus as your Lord and Savior, confess this prayer with me and you will be saved!

The Prayer of True Salvation

"Father, I come before your throne repenting for not understanding Your will You've planned for me since the foundation of the earth. Forgive me, for all of my trespasses I've committed against You as well as the Holy Spirit. I now acknowledge that I (insert your name) believe that Jesus died on the cross for my sins and was resurrected on the third day and has ascended to heaven, sitting at the right hand of God. I (insert your name) also acknowledge that Jesus is the only Way, the Truth and Life. I invite Jesus into my heart willingly to rest, rule and abide over the life He has given me. Endow me with your Holy Spirit that will lead and guide me in all ways of righteousness. In the mighty name of Jesus, I pray. Amen."

<u>Romans 10:9</u>
That if thou shalt confess with thy mouth the Lord Jesus, and shalt believe in thine heart that God hath raised him from the dead, thou shalt be saved.

Congratulations, you have accepted the greatest gift anyone could ever receive; salvation! Whether you are a new believer, have been newly converted or are re-dedicating your life back to Christ, it is with great honor to welcome you into the Kingdom of Heaven! I rejoice with the angels today for the immense change that's taking place in your life. I wish you much success on your future endeavors, and I declare that your latter rain will be greater than your former rain.

TAKE OFF

Take off the former behaviors of the old man, so that you can take flight (accelerate) in Christ!

Old things are passed away;
behold, all things are become new.

- 2 Corinthians 5:1

CHAPTER 3

Take Off the Old Man: Clothing the Pneu Creature

One thing we all have in common is that we have a past. We all have committed sinful acts that we're not proud of and created some stories that we don't care to share. For some reason, it's hard for people to move forward because they can't get past the former things that were present in their life at one time or another. Why is that? As I pondered on that question I began to think about the mindset of those whom have been abused either physically or verbally.

When a victim is abused, it creates an emotional attachment and puts a physiological fear within them. Once fear is present; it creates feelings of helplessness, dependency, and confinement to the abuser. The victim knows it's not a good situation; nonetheless, the abuser is all they know. The situation becomes natural and the victim perceives it as normal. Statistic show that it takes a victim seven times to leave the abuser because by the seventh time, the psychological fear breaks within them and they develop the courage to break the cycle.

For instance, in my teenage years before entering into adulthood, I did various things that I'm not proud of. My life was consumed with smoking, drinking, drugging, and I was possessed by the spirit of lust and fornication (sex). In the midst of operating in these spirits, it didn't register in my mind as wrong. From an intellectual perspective, it was normal and natural to do. After all, everybody else was doing it. I was living in iniquity but I went to church faithfully.

On a certain Sunday morning, I got up and went about my day as I normally do. I made up in my mind that I wasn't going to church that day, but I felt an urge to get to the house of God. As I was getting dressed, I could feel a presence I had never experienced before. The atmosphere was thick and I could literally feel *something* around me. As I looked back on that day, I now know it was the Holy Spirit. My heart was filled with so much conviction that I became heavy and wept uncontrollably. In spite of that, I still made it to church.

When I entered the sanctuary, it was as if God prepared the atmosphere specifically for me. With every word that was spoken, I knew God was calling me to change. Everything within me resisted. I must have gone to the bathroom a dozen times that day, because every time I felt the word convict me, I would go cry in the bathroom, wipe the tears from my eyes, and put back on the "I'm good face." As I returned back to my seat God continued to deal with me until I went to the altar and surrendered my life unto him.

At the altar, God spoke these words to my heart: "Your weeping is an expression of My heart towards you. Will I not leave the 99 for the one?" I began to weep even more. I always portrayed God as an entity that rules with an iron fist. I had never experienced His love and compassion until that moment.

When I left the altar, I was light, free and completely saved. To God be the Glory! The love and compassion of God broke the psychological fear within me and I was strengthened to break the cycle of continuous sin in my life. The ironic thing is, I really didn't know I wasn't saved until I became saved!

As the days and the weeks went by I was still excited in the Lord and my zeal was through the roof! I joined various departments and even became director over the youth and dance departments. All in all, I was content with being in the background.

The struggle came (at that time in my life) when I started to receive prophecies. I was invited to a church in Augusta, Georgia called Catch the Wind. The pastors began to prophesy and told me about all the wonderful acts God would have me perform and how I was ordained as a prophet to the nations. They even confirmed some things as well. When they finished prophesying it was 35 minutes later! From that point on, everywhere that I went, somebody had a word concerning me whether it was at the grocery store or while visiting a church. In no shape, form, or fashion am I writing this to boast, I'm going somewhere with this.

Earlier I mentioned that when I was in the world, I really couldn't see the sin because it was natural to me. When I heard the prophecies, they shined a light on my past and the former things began to condemn me. I no longer felt free or saved. I began to look at everything I wasn't and then the voice of the old nature began to speak, "God, do you know who I am? I was the alcoholic, the weed smoker, *and* the fornicator. Father, I was the master of manipulation." It didn't stop there, it turned into a woe is me session.

The memories began to overtake and flood my mind. Before I knew it, everything came to the surface—the hurt, the pain, being molested, the death of my father, feeling unwanted, etc. I couldn't imagine that God wanted to use me in this capacity. I was comfortable and didn't want to move outside the borders of familiarity. I didn't want the responsibility for what has been entrusted to me. What if I failed? What if I couldn't produce what was expected of me? These are the things that come to mind when you haven't taken off the old man. The old man likes to put you back in remembrance of the former things, hoping to lure you back into an unprofitable position.

Ephesians 4:21-23
21 If so be that ye have heard him, and have been taught by him, as the truth is in Jesus:
22 That ye put off concerning the former conversation the old man, which is corrupt according to the deceitful lusts;
23 And be renewed in the spirit of your mind;

The words "take off" are not just about removing something from a natural body. It includes removing bad behaviors and careless actions from your natural mind. The Bible says that the natural mind is carnal and is enmity (deep-rooted hatred) against God. Carnal is considered as: Dirty, lustful, fleshly, earthly, worldly.

The old nature desires to have you stuck! You may have known a person for over 10 years, but they are still doing the same thing from a decade ago! This is not an open rebuke or judgment, but this is what *stagnation* looks like.

It saddens my heart to see people stuck; especially, when you can look past a person's faults and see the potential and the type of life he or she could have if they developed the courage to break the cycle of negativity and poverty. Although my heart is sad to see a person in this situation, it also shows me the only thing that separates me from that person is the power of change that entered my life by the love of Christ. I was taught that whatever you've been delivered from, minister to those who have not overcome in that area. I quickly learned that not everyone will not receive you because they're focused more on the old man instead of the new creature.

Stagnation- the state or condition of being stagnant, or having stopped, as by ceasing to run or flow; state of inactivity.

"Stag" is derived from the word stagger meaning: to move or stand unsteadily, as if under a great weight. When you don't move forward, you are throwing a whole nation in a condition of unbalance. For so long people have looked at a nation as some distant place or a third-world country. While that may be true, a nation is also considered a descendent of people from your lineage or family line. If you make decisions according to the flesh, you will hinder the people that come behind you and not be an example for the people that God set before you.

Galatians 5:19-21
19 Now the works of the flesh are manifest, which are these; Adultery, fornication, uncleanness, lasciviousness,
20 Idolatry, witchcraft, hatred, variance, emulations, wrath, strife, seditions, heresies,
21 Envyings, murders, drunkenness, revellings, and such like: of the which I tell you before, as I have also told you in time past, that they which do such things shall not inherit the kingdom of God.

The reason why the old nature operates in these sins is because the old nature is linked to the god of this world. Satan wants you to forfeit your kingdom inheritance, which are the promises of God.

2 Corinthians 4:4
In whom the god of this world hath blinded the minds of them which believe not, lest the light of the glorious gospel of Christ, who is the image of God, should shine unto them.

So, if at any time you find yourself in these categories, God has given us specific instructions to be in His perfect will:

Romans 12:2
And be not conformed to this world: but be ye transformed by the renewing of your mind, that ye may prove what _is_ that good, and acceptable, and perfect, will of God.

1 John 1:9
If we confess our sins, he is faithful and just to forgive us our sins, and to cleanse us from all unrighteousness.

2 Chronicles 7:14

If my people, which are called by my name, shall humble themselves, and pray, and seek my face, and turn from their wicked ways; then will I hear from heaven, and will forgive their sin, and will heal their land.

Yes, it is that simple! All you have to do is submit and repent, knowing that you are a recipient of Romans 8:1 that declares:

"There is therefore now no condemnation to them which are in Christ Jesus, who walk not after the flesh, but after the Spirit. The spirit that brings change into our lives and break the psychological fear of moving forward and embracing our new beginning.

Clothing of the Pneu Creature

Now that the past is behind you, you can rejoice that you are joint heirs with Christ. Being confident of this very thing, that he which hath begun a good work in you will perform *it* until the day of Jesus Christ (Philippians 1:6). Being a pneu creature attests to the truth that God has given you a new birth, a new mind and a new character.

It's amazing to know that God found pleasure when He drew you out from among the heathen, preserved you, and blew His pneuma (breath of life) within you. In the process of the transformation, the kingdom was transferred to you as a believer.

You may live in this world, but you're a citizen of the Kingdom. This makes you an ambassador for Christ. Generally speaking, an ambassador is a respected representative acting on behalf of a nation. A role of an ambassador is to reflect the sovereignty of the one who sent you. In order to hold this position, you have to speak according to the Word of God, and not by what you see.

Earlier, I spoke about the old man and how I couldn't see the provision that God made for me due to my former situation. Now, I am glad to report that I am walking in the newness of life. I made a conscious decision that I wasn't going to wrestle with anything that couldn't bless me in the end.

Back in the day, there was a saying, "Don't test me." When I heard my mom say this, I knew that I had better sit down, because if I didn't it was about to go down! The other saying was, "You got it going on," describing that this person had a bright future, or had been favored in many areas in life. How I like to put it is, "You got some business about yourself."

I say to you this day, if your situation cannot bless you, don't let it test you. If it can bless you, withstand the test! I declare: The next time you say I have a lot going on in my life, know that it is because you have a lot going on!

Satan only goes after movement, progresssion and acceleration; he doesn't go after stagnation. Stagnation doesn't pose a threat to the kingdom of darkness. This is a new day to make your own personal declaration that you can confidently stand and walk in your newfound newness in life.

2 Corinthians 5:17

Therefore if any man *be* in Christ, *he is* a new creature: old things are passed away; behold, all things are become new.

Therefore if any man be in Christ: The word creature translates to new kind (Strong's *Concordance* G2537) signifying that the old nature no longer exists.

Old things are passed away: The former things have perished or disappeared, or the way you had previously done things.

Behold, all things are become new: See! God is establishing new things to bring them into existence.

Philippians 4:13
"I can do all things through Christ which strengtheneth me."

I can do all things: I have the power to achieve all things

Through Christ: The word "Christ" means the anointed one. The anointing gives you the ability to accomplish things that you originally cannot do on your own. It is success that's manifested and established by a different source other than yourself, and that source is Christ.

That strengtheneth me: It empowers, and causes you to believe that you can do all things!

It's wonderful to declare, but also to confirm the prophecies with Scripture. It empowers and encourages us to move forward in the things concerning God. Also, it makes us more appreciative of the transformation that took place in our lives.

As a pneu creature, there is a level of maturity we must possess. Let's face it, everybody will not celebrate your newness. You may lose some friends, may be talked about amongst your family, may have to give up some possessions, may be lied on and persecuted to some extent, but this is to be expected. When you allow the mind of Christ to be in you, carnal behavior is not an option, retaliation will no longer be an option, defending yourself is not an option. Truth will be your weapon against opposition.

Life Lesson: Once upon a time, I used to worry about what people thought about me. I was a people pleaser to the 10th power. I didn't understand why people disliked me. After all, I tried to meet the needs of everybody, even if it cost me. Speedily (can the church say amen?), I learned that people will celebrate you as long as it's benefiting them but when you give a sanctified NO, you are disloyal, unfaithful, and not privileged to be called friend.

If we don't die to our flesh daily, we'll allow behaviors such as these to pull us into a place of immaturity. When we put on the mind of

Christ; begin to think as He does and be wise in His eyes and not our own. There is an increase of joy and peace that I can testify to:

Proverbs 16:7
When a man's ways please the LORD, he maketh even his enemies to be at peace with him.

God has this amazing way of having your enemies bless you, even though their original intent was to harm you or even to assassinate your character. Allow the Lord of Peace to order your steps through every disappointment and every setback. The old has vanished, now behold: a new, fresh, advanced, right now anointing!

CHAPTER 4

Be it Unto Me
According to Thy Word

<u>Luke 1:26-38</u>
Be it unto me according to thy word.

As children of God, it's important that we read and study out the scriptures in the Bible. Joshua 1:8 tells us if we meditate on the Word day and night and do what is written, He will make our way prosperous and we will have good success! By studying we get a greater understanding of who God is and the will He has for our lives.

When you know your purpose through Scripture, it gives you the power to step into uncharted territories that you never treaded upon before. Studying scriptures builds your courage, your boldness and catapults your faith into a place of security of knowing. You can have faith in something or someone, but it may not necessarily be true. A *knowing* is an accurate truth that is connected to a Divine experience.

I've encountered storms in my life that were not God's will for me, but because I moved in logic and facts I was constantly revisiting the same mountain. Fact was a constant reminder that my situation wasn't going to change. Truth was the affirmation and declaration that I wasn't going to visit that mountain again!

My faith began to grow by leaps and bounds because of the great work He performed in my life. The more I know about our Lord and Savior, the more I embrace the knowing. I still have some trials and experiences; however, I know if God be for me who can be against me?

I still cry when I don't understand my process. My tears are not because I don't have hope, but the more I suffer I know that I will reign with Him in Glory! The suffering causes me to glorify Him and not deny Him. Through it all, we still must respond with "Thank You, Jesus" "I glorify You" "I worship and adore You." I've learned that the way we respond could either ensnare us and delay our blessings or it could align us with a great release.

Usually, when God is taking us through the process and He reveals to us the greater, we confer with flesh and blood (people). When others don't agree, we allow the opinion of those people to cloud our judgment. Instead of saying "Yes, Lord," we say "Let me pray about it first." In a subtle way, that's telling God we don't believe Him and we don't want the responsibility that comes along with the promise. That's not the response we want to give when we're entering into a season of harvest. So, what is the proper response? Let's look at the text below:

Luke 1:26-38
26 And in the sixth month the angel Gabriel was sent from God unto a city of Galilee, named Nazareth,

In the Jewish culture, the sixth month is considered the month of Elul that means "search" and "harvest." Gabriel's name means Man of God.

27 To a virgin espoused to a man whose name was Joseph, of the house of David; and the virgin's name was Mary.

Mary being a virgin symbolized that she was not tainted nor tampered with, but pure. This is what the Word of God does to us; it cleanses and purifies. Joseph names means "to add or give increase."

28 And the angel came in unto her, and said, Hail, thou that art highly favoured, the Lord is with thee: blessed art thou among women.

41

The salutation of Gabriel confirms that God specifically chose or elected Mary. To be chose, means we are appointed by God to the most exalted office conceivable.

> 29 **And when she saw him, she was troubled at his saying, and cast in her mind what manner of salutation this should be.**
> 30 **And the angel said unto her, Fear not, Mary: for thou hast found favour with God.**
> 31 **And, behold, thou shalt conceive in thy womb, and bring forth a son, and shalt call his name JESUS.**
> 32 **He shall be great, and shall be called the Son of the Highest: and the Lord God shall give unto him the throne of his father David:**
> 33 **And he shall reign over the house of Jacob for ever; and of his kingdom there shall be no end.**
> 34 **Then said Mary unto the angel, How shall this be, seeing I know not a man?**

The word *know* doesn't mean she did not know Joseph. She was espoused to him, but not yet married. *Know* means she was not yet intimate with Joseph.

35 **And the angel answered and said unto her, The Holy Ghost shall come upon thee, and the power of the Highest shall overshadow thee: therefore also that holy thing which shall be born of thee shall be called the Son of God.**

Often, we don't give enough credit to the Holy Ghost. In Christiandom, we have reduced the power of the Holy Ghost down to being a Keeper. He is more than a Keeper! The Holy Spirit leads and guides us into all truth and understanding. I love the translation of the complete Jewish Bible because it shows the power of the Holy Ghost. It says "The *Ruach HaKodesh* will come over you, the power of *Ha'Elyon* will cover you. Therefore, the holy child born to you will be called the Son of God.

36 **And, behold, thy cousin Elisabeth, she hath also conceived a son in her old age: and this is the sixth month with her, who was called barren.**
37 **For with God nothing shall be impossible.**
38 **And Mary said, Behold the handmaid of the Lord; be it unto me according to thy word. And the angel departed from her.**

Mary knew that Elizabeth was in a state of barrenness so to hear that her cousin was pregnant, she knew it was God. She no longer felt perplexed or troubled but agreed by responding, "Be it unto me according to thy word." Are you agreeing with the prophecies that have been spoken in your life or are you doubting? Are you taking God at his Word, or living in reality?

If we look closely at passages 36 and 37, we see that God has orchestrated a specific plan. The name Elizabeth means "oath of God" "pledge to God" and "God's promise" Notice that the promise (Elizabeth) was expecting too. In other words, what you are expecting is already expecting you! The promise has already been given, we just have to catch up with the promise. As the saints of old used to say, "What God has for you, is for you. The world didn't give it and the world can't take it away." The only requirement is to trust and believe.

Steps to Trusting God at His Word

1. Spend time with our Heavenly Father

Have you ever had a special friend or family member you loved to spend time with? You felt like you could be yourself completely and express things to them that others would not understand. The more you learned about them the more comfortable you became. The more you learned that person's character you began to trust them. It's no difference with our heavenly Father.

When we learn of God we can trust Him in all of His ways. Now-a-days, it's so easy to get distracted by our busy schedules so much that we merely try to work God into our agenda. We set appointments for our hair, nails, and even gym time. How often do we set aside time to be with God?

Did you know that God loves it when we worship? The Bible says, **"But the hour cometh, and now is, when the true worshippers shall worship the Father in spirit and in truth: for the Father seeketh such to worship him. God *is* a Spirit: and they that worship him must worship *him* in spirit and in truth** (John 4:23-24). Worship not only draws us closer to God, it provokes God's presence in our atmosphere to speak to us. This is the time during which God will release names for your businesses, vision for ministries, titles for books, and strategies to create wealth. That alone time with God also gives you the determination to fulfill all of the promises that God has placed in your hand. We want to make our heavenly Father proud.

2. We can do nothing without God

(John 15:5) Ok. As much as we love ourselves, we all have been guilty of moving in our own opinions, thoughts, and judgments. We all have made choices that brought us a great deal of frustration and disappointments. When we make decisions without God, we are removing Him as the Supreme authority in our lives, and we become the dictator. Next, comes trusting in our own counsel. To have great success, we must depend on God for all of our needs. We have to trust Him, in His infinite wisdom, to make our decisions.

Allow God to choose your friends and the clothes you wear. What does clothing have to do with it? It tells others a lot about you. See, God is so mindful of us that He would use what we wear to orchestrate divine connection. When you know that you're nothing without God, you look for divine connections and blessings because you're not trusting in your own ability. It's easy to declare "I give myself away" when you trust God with the life He has given you.

3. Be content (Philippians 4:11)

Wherever you may be at this point in your life, trust you are exactly where you need to be. The promise is not predicated on your "right now."

You may be in a mountaintop experience or in a valley of decision; either way, God speaks in both situations.

There will come a time during this birthing process you're going to need finances and favor. There will also be times when it looks like you lack both, but when you take God at His Word, it reassures you that He is yet faithful.

4. Pray without ceasing

(1 Thessalonians 5:17) Pray, pray, pray! We can never pray too much. Prayer is the strength of the foundation that you build upon. For example, when a carpenter is building a house, the most important feature of the house is the foundation. The foundation determines the height, width, and the weight of a structure. If there are defects and mistakes in the foundation, the more the carpenter builds, the more the defects grow. If the carpenter chooses to ignore the defects, the structure will be useless. He may complete the house and it can look good inside and out, but as soon as a storm comes or major opposition surfaces, the house will not be able to withstand the test. Make sure that what you are building is strong and not a faulty foundation. Know that what you're building will be able to withstand any storm,

backlash, backbiting, haters, or traditions, just to name a few.

Lord I Believe, But Help My Unbelief

In life, God gives us our own experiences that attest to His goodness and mercy. I have been in situations where I knew it wasn't anybody but God that could have brought me out.

In the Bible, there are numerous stories about how God healed and raised people from the dead. Clearly it can be done; however, I never seen it performed in real life, so I had some unbelief there. I knew it could happen to other people, but things like that don't happen to me. That was my mindset 7 years ago. Then God gave me an experience that caused me to take Him at His Word.

It was time for me to give birth to my last son. I got up that morning, everything was great, and I headed to the hospital. The staff prepped me for surgery and gave me an epidural. In the process of the nurse giving me an epidural, I started feeling light headed and then the strangest thing happened… I could literally feel my spirit leaving my body! I told the nurse, "You are giving me to much medicine. I can't breathe." She responded, "Oh, that's the way it supposed to feel. Don't worry, you'll be ok." I knew that something was wrong. I looked at my husband and said, "If something happens to me, just know that I love you and the children."

They laid me back and proceeded with the C-section. My son was born, and I immediately flatlined. According to the doctor, my husband was rushed out the room and they began to resuscitate me. During that procedure, I had an out-of-body experience and I could see the doctors trying to revive me. Although I saw stories on TV talking about events like this, I didn't think it was possible. Ten-and-a-half minutes later, the Lord performed a miracle! From that day forward, I no longer needed help with my unbelief.

There will be times in your life that you don't understand what God is doing, but He has given you a testimony and the testimonies of others to teach you how to trust Him. Let's look at one of the most popular passages in the Bible that people use to examine unbelief or a lack of faith:

Matthew 14:22-33
22 And straightway Jesus constrained his disciples to get into a ship, and to go before him unto the other side, while he sent the multitudes away.

23 **And when he had sent the multitudes away, he went up into a mountain apart to pray: and when the evening was come, he was there alone.**

24 **But the ship was now in the midst of the sea, tossed with waves: for the wind was contrary.**

25 **And in the fourth watch of the night Jesus went unto them, walking on the sea.**

26 **And when the disciples saw him walking on the sea, they were troubled, saying, It is a spirit; and they cried out for fear.**

27 **But straightway Jesus spake unto them, saying, Be of good cheer; it is I; be not afraid.**

29 **And he said, Come. And when Peter was come down out of the ship, he walked on the water, to go to Jesus.**

30 **But when he saw the wind boisterous, he was afraid; and beginning to sink, he cried, saying, Lord, save me.**

31 **And immediately Jesus stretched forth his hand, and caught him, and said unto him, O thou of little faith, wherefore didst thou doubt?**

Like Peter, we literally hear His voice and we start out in faith, but the more resistance we encounter from the storm can cause a person to lose focus.

Personally, I don't believe he was afraid to walk on water. If that's the case, he wouldn't have got out of the boat. I believe the storm distracted him, and he realized that he was doing something that was defying the odds and gravity. Outside of Jesus Christ, he's the only one who experienced walking on water.

If you'll be truthful with yourself, the reason you won't move forward is because you don't see your yourself moving in a greater capacity. You don't see yourself as a millionaire or a business owner. You don't see yourself buying a house or driving what you desire to drive. You don't see yourself healing the sick, raising the dead or declaring the works of the Lord because you're reflecting on everything you believe you're not.

Today, believe you're the one Jesus is bidding to come forth. He's making you a miraculous experience that will give you the courage to keep pressing towards the mark. That season of keeping your head above water is over. Now it's time to walk on it! Walk the walk, talk the talk! Don't block the haters, let them be your elevator to success.

Expect the Great!

"Now unto him that is able to do exceeding abundantly above all that we ask or think, according to the power that worketh in us."

CHAPTER 5

Expect the Great

You produce what you expect. What are you expecting God to do? Even in your approach to life, are you believing God for the abundant blessing or the just enough blessing?

My approach use to be, "God, as long as my bills are paid and food is in my house, I'm ok." Guess what? I got exactly what I asked for. One day I got tired of living from paycheck to paycheck—it wasn't enough to break even! Then, I pondered on this question: If I could ask for the least and it's provided, how much more would He provide if I asked for the greatest?

In Christiandom, we have become comfortable with religious sayings that are not biblically correct! "Father, if You never do another thing for me, You have already done enough!" Now, I have been guilty of saying this in the past, but no more. I understand why people say it; to them it's showing a sense of humbleness and contentment. However, that is not the will of God for your life. Tradition has taught us that we will receive our mansion and good fortune in heaven. Yes, we do have a mansion in heaven; however, it's God's desire that we eat the good of the land in the land of the living!

When you sow, whether with tithes and offerings or being a financial blessing to someone, you are sowing into your promise. For many years, I've heard when you give tithes and offerings they do not always come back in financial ways. They can come in other forms, like shielding you from car accidents, sickness, bad health and diseases.

Side Bar: We don't pay tithes, we cheerfully give what is required of us. The blessing is in the offering. The offering is tied to your relationship with God.

Psalm 121:7
The LORD shall preserve thee from all evil: he shall preserve thy soul.

Protection is already promised to you. That is activated out of your obedience. Let me let you in on a little secret... When a farmer plants oranges he doesn't expect a harvest of apples because the seed that was planted was an orange seed. When you sow financially, you reap back a financial harvest with favor to bring forth the promises.

3 John 1:2
"Beloved, I wish above all things that thou mayest prosper and be in health, even as thy soul prospereth."

We can't speak things out of traditions of men or denominations; we have to speak according to God's Word. He is such a covenant keeper that He gives us an opportunity to put Him back in remembrance of what He said He'll do for us.

God can do the miraculous in your life; however, it's released according to your faith. Your faith agrees with who you are and strengthens you for the assignment that is placed before you. It prepares you for the greater work. John 14:12 says, "Verily, verily, I say unto you, He that believeth on me, the works that I do shall he do also; and greater works than these shall he do; because I go unto my Father." We ought to rejoice that Jesus is sitting on the right hand of the Father! He is expecting us to do greater works! By Jesus leaving, our inheritance was released, which is the will of God.

Will- A will or testament is a legal declaration by which a person, the testator, names one or more persons to manage his or her estate and provides for the distribution of his or her property at death. You are literally an heir and a successor of Jesus Christ, and the Kingdom has been transferred to you.

There is nothing slack nor lacking in the Kingdom; only greatness resides in the Kingdom. The word **great** means: an extent, amount, or intensity considerably above the normal or average. Greatness will never produce under average or normal. Greatness produces the willpower and determination to birth the promises of God.

In the book of Genesis, God did a good work with creation. From day 1 to day 5, God expressed it was good. On day 6, God expressed, indeed it was very good. Additionally, authority, power and dominion was given to mankind. Father loves us so much that He's given us these three tools that would supersede the "good" he created.

You and I have no excuse not to expect the great; it's basically given to us. We weren't born with silver spoons in our mouths but God has handed us the tools we need to succeed on a silver platter! This is the time not to talk about it, but go forth in power and demonstration.

Perception

<u>Hebrews 5:14</u>
But strong meat belongeth to them that are of full age, even those who by reason of use have their senses exercised to discern both good and evil.

Perception is a major key to your spiritual and natural success. The 5 senses also play a key role in how you perceive things, whether it be physically or spiritually. Have you ever seen something that seemed so real, but later on discovered that it wasn't true? Have you ever heard negativity about a person and once you meet them, they're nothing like the rumor you heard? That's why it's important to exercise your senses and not be persuaded with the opinions or actions of others.

When you are easily persuaded, it can potentially cloud your judgment and cause you to believe that you can't obtain the promise. While standing in the spirit of expectation, there is something called haters that expect you to fail. Some people will build you up in public, and demolish you in private. There will be family members that don't support or sow into your vision. These are situations that could easily break you or cause a breakdown, but it all goes back to how you perceive it. You can either wallow in self-pity, despair or cry woe is me, or you can perceive that God is doing a new thing. He allowed people not to sow, so you can depend on Him.

Truth is, we use our senses in everyday life. Whatever is in our atmosphere will register to the brain that is stimulated from our senses. Let's look at the following functions:

1. **Sight:** *The power of seeing; the faculty of vision, or of perceiving objects by the instrumentality of the eyes.* In the natural we have vision, which gives us the ability to see things before us. Spiritually, when God gives us vision, He's showing us ordained events that will come or be fulfilled in its proper season.

Numbers Chapter 13 contains a wonderful analogy about natural and spiritual vision. Moses was instructed to send one man from every tribe of Israel to spy out the land of Canaan. The men were responsible for bringing back a report about the land.

Upon returning back to the tribes, they gave a report stating that the land truly flowed with milk and honey. They even brought back evidence of the harvest of grapes, but some of the men focused their natural vision on the people of the land, and didn't focus on the promise. They concentrated on the perception of the people being strong and fortified. They even declared that the people of the land were giants and they were grasshoppers in their own sight! However, Caleb stood and said, "Let us go up at once, and possess it; for we are well able to overcome it." Here is a classic example of many hearing the same word but some didn't mix it with faith. On this journey, you will encounter giants in your promised land. You can either see the giant or the promise. Will you have an experience of defeat or a Caleb experience?

2. **Hearing:** *To use the power of perceiving sound; to perceive or apprehend by the ear; to attend; to listen.* Be careful who you lend your ear to. Did you know when we speak, it's a combination of tones and sounds that create words? Sound has the ability to shape our minds and thoughts. Some of the functions are: Thinking, feeling and wanting.

3. **Taste:** *To have perception, experience, or enjoyment; to partake; as, to taste of nature's bounty.* Oh, taste and see that the Lord is good! Have you ever known someone who raved about their sweet potato pie, and insisted you had to try it? They may have added these famous words: "Girl,

this is gonna make you slap yo mama!" Your response is prompted by their excitement. "Ok, make me one!" You get this pie. It looks good, smells good, and now it's time to taste. You realize from that taste test that you will not be slapping yo mama or the dog! The moral of the story is, what might taste good to someone else may not taste good to you.

Your perception may be different from someone else's perception. Your vision will differ greatly from someone else's vision. Your promise will not be just like someone else's promises. When you know this, it helps you deal with people who say, "If it were me, I would do it like this…" or, "I would build it like that…" What they're saying could make perfect sense, but they're speaking from their own experience versus you speaking from an experience that has been cultivated from your relationship with God. I'm not saying don't take counsel from people concerning business or ministries that are to come, just make sure you are taking counsel from the sons and daughters in the gospel and not Judas!

4. **Smell:** *To detect or perceive, as if by the sense of smell; to scent out.* Smell is linked to your discernment. It gives us the ability to identify a situation before we see it. If something has

caught on fire, we'll detect the aroma of smoke before we see the actual fire.

Smell also warns us not to make unfavorable decisions. Have you ever heard the expression, "Something smells fishy?" This particular phrase insinuates that there is something suspicious going on around someone. It could be a person's character or having ulterior motives.

We are in the season of divine connections. It's important to know who God is linking you with. An unfavorable decision would be to link with someone because they have a nice house or drive the latest Mercedes and "look" prosperous. The fruit is not always in material possessions. Now, there is nothing wrong with having a nice house and the latest car, because I desire a 5-bedroom home with an Audi A6. Father said that if we delight ourselves in the Lord (Provider), He shall give us the desires of our hearts; however, material possessions should not be the motive of gaining success.

When divine connections are ordained for you, you don't have to seek for opportunities, connections will gravitate towards you! The only thing you have to do is use the sense of smell to perceive who's the connection or the professional frustrater (enemies of God).

5. **Touch:** *To perceive by the sense of feeling. Act or power of exciting emotion.* Luke 8:43-48 There was a certain woman dealing with an issue of blood for 12 years. She went to all the physicians in her land, but yet she was not made whole. Now, here comes Jesus and He's surrounded by multitudes of people. She was so determined that she pushed through the crowd by crawling to touch the hem of His garment. "Who touched me?" Jesus responded. I can imagine lots of people touching Him that day, but it was something about her touch that caused the virtue (power) to project from His body.

She fell down before him and stated the reason why she touched Him. Jesus responded, "Daughter, be of good comfort: thy faith hath made thee whole; go in peace." Note to self: stop touching things and reaching out to people that cannot bless you!

You have exhausted your time, energy, and resources. Just like this woman, it has to be a desperate situation to crawl past the haters, the opinions of people, the embarrassment, the way it used to be, and reach out and touch the hem of His garment. My question to you is, how bad do you want it?

Are your expectations based off what you can see, or what you can't see? If you can see it, would it really be expectation? Expectation is linked with your faith and faith is linked with works. Expectation puts works into action that confirm you believe with every vision, dream, and prophecy that has been spoken over your life. Your expectation has to be determined, willing, relentless, and fervent, because the same word you're going after, the enemy is going after as well.

It's the enemy job to stop your expectations from coming into fruition. If you stand firm on the Word of God, no plot or plan of the enemy will prevail against the Word because His Word cannot return back to Him void! Since He is not a man that He should lie, He will watch over His Word to perform it. Jesus is expecting you to do greater works.

I speak greater ministry, greater anointing, greater prayer, greater business and witty ideas. I charge you to expect the great, because the greater is expecting you!

John 14:12
Verily, verily, I say unto you, He that believeth on me, the works that I do shall he do also; and greater *works* than these shall he do; because I go unto my Father.

CHAPTER 6

Intimacy

What comes to mind when you think about the word **intimacy**? Naturally, many people relate intimacy as sexually-oriented or a feeling that pleases the natural body. Intimacy goes beyond sexual or physical contact. Intimacy requires for an individual to let their guards down and share their hopes, dreams, aspirations, hurts, fears, and desires with someone other than themselves.

Intimacy allows a person to get to know you further than what they see on the outside. It is an essential part of any relationship, whether it be a best friend or spouse. Intimacy is designed to create a union and oneness interchangeably with one another.

Intimacy- *Close familiarity or friendship; closeness. A private cozy atmosphere.*

Synonyms: *Togetherness, confidence, attachment*

Types of Intimacy

Emotional intimacy is normally attached to how you feel. How you feel is usually prompted by what took place in your day. Were you happy, sad, mad, or angry? Whatever the case may be, you will respond according to your mood or atmosphere. The goal of emotional intimacy is having you truthfully share how you feel. For instance, if you're sad, don't perpetrate as if you're happy. If you're mad, don't lie and say you're sad! What this does is open up a line of communication that moves you forward in the realm of trust.

Cognitive intimacy is when an individual becomes comfortable sharing their ideas and desires with one another. It's easier for them to open up and express the deeper sentiments of their hearts and the conversation is more detailed and thorough. As a result, that individual begins to listen intently to the ideas and the desires of the other person, which will lead into developing a relationship on a greater level.

Disclaimer: I'm not saying everyone you come in contact with to be intimate or share your innermost thoughts. Once again, intimacy is not about sex! I simply explained intimacy from a natural perspective to give a greater understanding of spiritual intimacy and how we ought to entreat the Father, Son, and the Holy Spirit.

Spiritual Intimacy with God

When I was a teenager I couldn't wait to become of age to date. As I looked around me, people looked happy, in love and excited about companionship. You couldn't tell me that the birds weren't chirping on the window pane. I was young naive and ready to jump into the pool of love with both feet in!

I longed for intimacy. I wanted someone to tell me I was beautiful, or even cute. I wanted to feel loved and appreciated. So, when the opportunity presented itself I made myself available. It was everything I thought I wanted, but something was missing. Even with hearing what I wanted to hear, a void would be filled temporarily; however, after a while I would feel empty.

It went from being satisfied to not enough. Since it wasn't enough, like the old saying goes, I began to look for love in all the wrong places. Smoking weed became my happiness and alcohol became my love.

As I stated earlier in the book, I remember crying out to God, telling Him that I was tired of the way I was and the situations I'd gotten myself into. As I look back on that day, I understand that the feeling of incompleteness was not from a lack of people or things, it was from the lack of intimacy with God.

James 4:8
Draw nigh to God, and he will draw nigh to you. Cleanse your hands, ye sinners; and purify your hearts, ye double minded.

Psalm 145:18
The Lord is nigh unto all them that call upon him, to all that call upon him in truth.

One thing the scriptures above have in common is God's desire to draw nigh unto us. Even so, we have to put forth the effort and show interest that we want to get to know God in all His ways. We have to be willing to invite the Father, Son, and Holy Spirit into every aspect of our lives.

Once we can commit, God will honor our actions. For example, when a person gets married or engaged they want to know everything about their mate. Where are you from? What do you do for a living? Some people will go as far as pulling a background check just to make sure a person is really who they say they are. That's the type of desperation and hunger that prompts God to move and draw closer to us.

Intimacy is a tool for Kingdom-minded people. You can't be Kingdom without the tool of intimacy. A tool is also known as an implement, which means you have to apply an action for a particular purpose.

Moses utilized the tool of intimacy with God. In Exodus 33, it references Moses pitching a tent called the "tent of meeting." The tent of meeting was a portable sanctuary where God met with His people. When Moses entered the tabernacle, a pillar of cloud would come down and stay at the entrance while God spoke with him. He was so in union with God that the Bible tells us that God spoke with Moses face-to-face, like a friend would.

So how exactly did Moses develop this relationship? The answer is found in verse 13:

Now therefore, I pray thee, if I have found grace in thy sight, shew me now thy way, that I may know thee, that I

may find grace in thy sight: and consider that this nation is thy people.

The keywords in this verse are: "Shew me now thy way, that I may know thee." Moses developed a relationship by desiring to know the ways of the Father. Just like Moses, if you desire to know the ways of the Father, you will find favor in the sight of God; meaning, you have gained approval and acceptance. Now you are entitled to the benefits and the blessings, that produces His grace, mercy and His protection. God's response was in verse 14:

And he said, My presence shall go with thee, and I will give thee rest.

In your alone time, read the entire chapter of Exodus 33. You'll see that Moses was given an assignment to lead the children of Israel to the promised land. During that particular journey, God expressed to Moses that He would send an angel before him to drive out all the inhabitants of that land (Canaan) for the children of Israel to possess.

God's response was not merely a statement, but God honored his request and assured him that no longer would He send a created being (Angel) to fight on His behalf, but His very presence would surely be with him every step of the way. Since Moses actions were acceptable, the promises of God (His presence and rest) was extended to the Israelites. This was all due to Moses utilizing the tool of intimacy.

When you put intimacy into action, it will cause God's presence to abide around you. He will serve as your protector and also a shield. A shield could be known as someone or something that protects you from danger. It is also a type of armor that block attacks, swords, and arrows from your enemies.

Exodus 14:14
The LORD shall fight for you, and ye shall hold your peace.

When we try to fight our own battles, it distracts us from our purpose. It exhausts us and brings with it overwhelming feelings of frustration. That's why God has given us instructions to rest in Him. This rest allows us to remain sober-minded and diligent towards the things of God. It shifts our focus from everyday issues we face in our lives and shines the spotlight on the solution.

Your issues may not be my issues and my issues may not be your issues. One thing I have come to know is, when we allow ourselves to learn the attributes and characteristics of God, we won't focus on the problem because we are unified with the One who has the answer to solve it.

Intimacy Through Prayer

To continually have a relationship with God, prayer is essential and necessary. Earlier, we noted the importance of communication with God through the life of Moses. Now we'll explore what it means to petition or make our request made known unto Him.

When I was a babe in Christ, I thought that prayer was solely communication with God. My prayer life consisted of saying my prayers in the morning and before I went to bed. I'd pray for people I knew or family members and that was it. In my mind, I'd done my duty for that day.

Since I prayed, I thought, "Huh, I should join the intercessory prayer movement at church." I started attending the prayer classes regularly. I learned besides prayer being a communication, it is an art and an unselfish act of worship. No matter if you're kneeling or standing, in private or in public, your petitions have to be made in faith.

Philippians 4:6-7

6 **Be careful for nothing; but in every thing by prayer and supplication with thanksgiving let your requests be made known unto God.**
7 **And the peace of God, which passeth all understanding, shall keep your hearts and minds through Christ Jesus.**

Why does the scripture tell us to be careful for nothing? Because we are aware that we live in a world where calamity and struggle happen, but the cares of the world should not bring us to place of anxiousness. We cannot begin to depend on our own abilities or manipulate our own blessings. God has given us an antidote to counteract every situation or circumstance. Naturally, a fireman will tell you if a fire breaks out: **S**top **D**rop and **R**oll. Spiritually, I will tell you: When the storms of life arise, remember to PST…

Pray (earnestly, forwardness)
Supplication (asking for favor from God)
Thanksgiving (giving of thanks in all things)

When you move in PST, God promises to release peace that will keep your heart and your mind through the power of Christ Jesus. The word "through" is just not a fill-in word. If you study the Word *through*, you'll understand why everything that is of importance or significance has to be done "through" Christ. Let's explore other scriptures that have "through" in them:

Philippians 4:19
For I know that this shall turn to my salvation <u>through</u> your prayer, and the supply of the Spirit of Jesus Christ,

Philippians 4:13
I can do all things <u>through</u> Christ who strengthens me.

Romans 8:36-37
As it is written, For thy sake we are killed all the day long; we are accounted as sheep for the slaughter. Nay, in all these things we are more than conquerors <u>through</u> him that loved us.

Ephesians 4:4-6
There is one body, and one Spirit, even as ye are called in one hope of your calling; One Lord, one faith, one baptism, One God and Father of all, who is above all, and <u>through</u> all, and in you all.

God is showing us that every decision, idea, gift, and anointing can only operate if we are in Christ. Let's explore the definition of through.

Through- *moving in one side and out of the other side of* (an opening, channel, or location). *Continuing in time toward completion of* (a process or period).

Operating in PST opens a portal to heaven. Your natural body may be in an earth realm, but your spirit is in a different location (3rd heaven). In the Spirit, you'll see exactly what God has concerning you and the Spirit will make intercession for you accordingly to what the Spirit has seen. A spiritual filtration will take place. As the Spirit is praying through Christ, Christ will move through you.

Remember, intimacy with God can't take place in the natural. Intimacy can only be achieved in the Spirit. The goal is to rely on the Holy Spirit because, being humanoids, we can ask and seek God for the wrong reason or even personal gain.

<u>James 4:3</u>
Ye ask, and receive not, because ye ask amiss, that ye may consume *it* upon your lusts.

From the Scripture, we can gather that the word "amiss" means wrong or improper. While studying the word amiss, I was surprised by its other meanings: *miserable, sick people, or to be sick, diseased and grievous.* As I pondered on the meanings, I wondered could sickness and disease be the results of approaching God wrong or selfishly? Are the infirmities working in the natural body a result of improper communication and fellowship with God? I'm not insinuating that infirmities and sickness are directly from God; however, as people we can become so anxious and impatient when we encounter storms or suffer loss that we accuse God during the process.

There is an account in the book of Numbers Chapter 21, verses 4-6 where the Israelites spoke against God and Moses because of the shortage of food and water. They approached God with complaining and murmuring. In return, fiery serpents (snakes) were sent out to bite the people. It may have been a shortage of food and water but that moment should not have compared to where God had brought them from.

Our testimony will not be like the Israelites! When you open your eyes on a day-to-day basis, it may seem that there is a shortage of finances, a shortage of help, or limited support, but true intimacy through prayer allows the individual to reflect on what God has already done. Travail in prayer for what He will release in you that will reflect that He lives in you! Once God can see His Son revealed in you, you are in a Kingdom authority position to utter your petition before the throne.

John 14:13-14
13 **And whatsoever ye shall ask in my name, that will I do, that the Father may be glorified in the Son.**
14 **If ye shall ask any thing in my name, I will do it.**

1 John 5:14-15
14 **And this is the confidence that we have in him, that, if we ask any thing according to his will, he heareth us:**
15 **And if we know that he hear us, whatsoever we ask, we know that we have the petitions that we desired of**

These scriptures will be fulfilled in your life once Jesus can say that He knows you—not just by name, but in a more intimate way. To prove this statement is true let's look at the next scripture:

<u>Jeremiah 1:5</u>
Before I formed thee in the belly I knew thee; and before thou camest forth out of the womb I sanctified thee, and I ordained thee a prophet unto the nations.

Here God is expressing to Jeremiah that He knew him beforehand; meaning, he was literally with Him in heavenly places.

The Bible tells us it is first natural then spiritual. Naturally intimacy must take place first before a seed is released in the womb, so this scripture would be the spiritual side of the natural revelation. Today, you are like the seed that is planted in a spiritual womb that will grow and come forth in due season by water and of the Spirit. Let your intimate prayers be the foundation of your affirmation that will carry you to destinations to proclaim restoration to all nations! ~Selah~

Intimacy Through Worship

On any given Sunday morning, you may hear a Pastor or worship leader say, "Let's worship

Him (God)." For some, the first reaction is to lift up their hands as a sign of reverence and honor. For others, it's a sign of surrender and submission. The Bible says let everything that has breath praise the Lord, meaning that everyone can participate in praise, but it takes a special kind of person to go forth in worship.

<u>Psalm 150:6</u>
Let every thing that hath breath praise the LORD. Praise ye the LORD.

<u>John 4:24</u>
God is a Spirit: and they that worship him must worship him in spirit and in truth.

The difference between these scriptures is one is a commandment and the other is relationship. Psalm 150:6 is a commandment for everything that has been created in heaven and in earth. It's not an option or a feeling predicated upon emotions where you get to decide if you feel like doing it or not.

Worship is honorable because that person is making a conscious decision to seek the face of God. There's no kicking, screaming, pumping and priming. It's prompted by a desire and a longing that a person has to be in the presence of the Almighty One. I believe true worship is stemmed from the perception of worth to that particular believer.

Worth
1. equivalent in value to the sum or item specified.
2. the value equivalent to that of someone or something under consideration; the level at which someone or something deserves to be valued or rated.

Synonyms: *benefit, advantage, virtue, profit, help, aid, price, value*

Looking over the definition, it states "item specified." An *item* is equated to a thing, and *specified* is to identify something clearly.

If God has brought you out of any sort of turmoil, confusion, trouble or chaos, worship should permeate your atmosphere because you can clearly identify the worthiness of our Almighty God! Let me let you in on a little secret: even if He decided not to deliver you, there is still a promise in worshipping Him just for who He is!

Exodus 23:25-26 (MSG)
But you—you serve your God and he'll bless your food and your water. I'll get rid of the sickness among you; there won't be any miscarriages nor barren women in your land. I'll make sure you live full and complete lives.

The word "serve" is used interchangeably with the word worship.

Deuteronomy 10:12-13 (MSG)
12-13 So now Israel, what do you think God expects from you? Just this: Live in his presence in holy reverence, follow the road he sets out for you, love him, serve God, your God, with everything you have in you, obey the commandments and regulations of God that I'm commanding you today—live a good life.

Colossians 3:23-24
Whatever you do, work at it with all your heart, as working for the Lord, not for human masters, since you know that you will receive an inheritance from the Lord as a reward. It is the Lord Christ you are serving.

CHAPTER 7

Don't Abort Your B.A.B.Y.

This book has been designed to inspire, uplift, and redirect your life towards the greater purpose. Now, let's get real… No matter how much someone speaks truth or positivity over your life, it all comes down to what you believe. Are you going to hold fast to the promise, or will the responsibility of the promise cause you to abort it?

In the U.S.A., the abortion rates are off the charts. Though women have abortions for a number of reasons (Disclaimer: I do not believe in abortion), one of the reasons is due to the individual not wanting to take care of the responsibility. When they think about the long-term investment and the time it requires to nurture and support a baby, fear kicks in. God has not given us a spirit of fear, but of power, and love, and of a sound mind.

Fear is manifested by the enemy and the sole purpose for fear is to attach a negative thought to it. Fear plus a negative thought equals an easy way out! If you're not careful; that particular mindset can hinder you from bringing your spiritual baby to full-term status.

The "easy way out" is a trap to keep you where you are, and block you from going where you need to be. It provides a way of fleeing from the things that have been ordained to pull your character, strength and endurance from within. It turns you into a coward who sings the "I could have, would have, should have" song. God hasn't called you into the position of a coward, but a position of an overcomer!

We as people have taken the easy way out for too long. The time is **now**, to go into the enemy's camp and take your possessions.

Ezekiel 36:2 (CJB)
Adonai ELOHIM says: "The enemy is boasting over you, 'Ha! Even the ancient high places are ours now!'"

The adversary is sitting back taking pleasure in you not moving forward towards your destiny. The enemy is not worried about you talking about your dreams and aspirations; it's when you start moving in the direction God intended.

While you're on this journey, he'll throw everything in his arsenal including the kitchen sink at you to keep you confused and stagnant. That's when you have to be convinced and persuaded that the blessing you are carrying is placed within you directly by God.

The Bible tells us there is no male or female, in Him, so no matter if you're a boy or girl, man or woman, you have to consider yourself the modern-day Mary that has been chosen to bring forth a deliverer. When I say deliverer, I'm not speaking in terms of a Savior. God sent Jesus to fulfill that assignment. The created being that is in your spiritual womb will deliver you from the bondage of Egypt and from the lack of Lo-debar. The creation is sent to do what it's designed to do, and that is create!

Romans 8:19
For the earnest expectation of the creature waiteth for the manifestation of the sons of God.

Romans 8:22
For we know that the whole creation groaneth and travaileth in pain together until now.

The earth is waiting for you, the earth is waiting for me, the earth is waiting for the church to walk in sonship and exercise our dominion. One night as I was going over the scriptures above, I asked God, "Why is the creature waiting for the sons of God and why is the earth moaning and groaning?" When Adam fell, not only did it affect mankind, it affected the earth as well. The earth is referred to as "her" and it's suffering from a type of pain that is equated to childbirth. As the body of Christ, we have been redeemed by the blood of Jesus, but the earth has not been redeemed by us!

Redeem- gain or regain possession of; recover, reclaim.

Genesis 1:26
And God said, Let us make man in our image, after our likeness: and let them have dominion over the fish of the sea, and over the fowl of the air, and over the cattle, and over all the earth, and over every creeping thing that creepeth upon the earth.

This is the commandment that was given to us and it shall be fulfilled through the promise. It is our responsibility to be fruitful, multiply, subdue and replenish. That is to say, what you are expecting is already expecting you! Allow the created being to reach full-term so you can see and witness the full potential of the promise.

Created (create)- *bring something into existence; produce, build, construct.*

Being- *life, existence, reality, actuality.*

The promise within your spiritual womb will produce, build, and construct a life of freedom for you, your family, and your children's children. Everything that has been promised to you will no longer be a dream or unfulfilled prophecy, but it will be a reality! You've seen the greater through your spiritual eyes. Now, it's time to behold it in the natural! Stay the course and do not abort your:

B Belief
A Anointing
B Belt of truth
Y Yahweh

Normally, I would expound on the words or give a definition but I want you to take it upon yourself to study the scriptures related to each word. I found that if you study the scriptures for yourself; it'll stick with you and forever resonate in your heart. Once you've studied, take a piece of paper and write down what it means to you. I pray what you've written down will open the eyes of your understanding on an even greater level concerning your destiny and promise.

At the beginning of this book I congratulated you on expecting, but what you do from here will determine your due date. I charge you to be the best version of you! Go, grow, conquer and complete!

CHAPTER 8

Labor Pains

And let us not be weary in well doing: for in due season we shall reap, if we faint not.

Our labor is not in vain. As the writer of this book, I can identify with labor pains. Many years ago, God revealed to me businesses and ministries, and books that I didn't pursue because I tried to avoid the labor process.

I have had numerous witty inventions and ideas that God has given me, but I released them to others that were already in business or successful. I was great at bringing other people's visions to pass, but flopped on my own. I continually procrastinated until one day God showed me a vision of where I was then and where I was supposed to be in Him. Because I lacked willpower and discipline, I was stuck and didn't even know it.

I've heard many times in Christiandom that wherever you are in life, that's where God wants you to be; however, the vision God showed me confirmed that that's not always true! God can have a destination for us, but if we keep taking alternate routes we will delay our time of arrival. God is gracious and merciful as we eventually make it to our destinations. So, in this vision, I already had the 5-bedroom home, my ministry was thriving by leaps and bounds and this book you're currently reading was empowering people to get out of impoverished situations. However, that was not my reality. I had to get to the root of why I was avoiding the labor process. Could it have been fear? Was I scared of succeeding? Was I afraid of failing? Truth is, I feared the responsibility.

I discovered it is easier to help others bring their visions to pass since I didn't have to nurture it or take on the maintenance of the vision. I had to humble myself and repent for trying to take the easy route. I was not being a diligent steward over what was entrusted to me.

After the repenting, crying and snotting (God whooped me good), I immediately got up and brushed myself off. I looked into the mirror and said to myself "April just because you delayed the promise doesn't mean that God change His mind about the promise." Not more than 20 hours later, He confirmed His Word through prophetic teaching.

I am a witness that there are times during the labor process when we will experience hurt and pain, but there is no way of stopping the process. In the natural sense, when a woman experiences pain during the labor process, it's confirmation that her baby is due to arrive soon. Spirituality when we go through pain, it's confirmation that the promise is due to arrive soon.

This is not the time to think about why you didn't abort, or put your promise up for adoption. This is the opportune time to rejoice in the pain because it's fulfilling something in you that you didn't know about yourself. It shows you how strong you are and what you can handle, versus what you said you couldn't bear. The pain is present to build your faith through every test, trial, and tribulation so that the glory of God may be revealed in you.

Romans 5:1-5
1 **Therefore being justified by faith, we have peace with God through our Lord Jesus Christ:**
2 **By whom also we have access by faith into this grace wherein we stand, and rejoice in hope of the glory of God.**
3 **And not only so, but we glory in tribulations also: knowing that tribulation worketh patience;**

4 And patience, experience; and experience, hope:
5 And hope maketh not ashamed; because the love of God is shed abroad in our hearts by the Holy Ghost which is given unto us.

The Holy Ghost will teach you to persevere through the stretching, the cramps and the contractions. You have power to endure the labor process. No more taking the easy way out, wishful thinking, or being a legend in your own mind.

It's time to take your eyes and attention off of the hell-e-vision (television) and place your eyes on the harvest! Never look at the success of others and think they've got it made or have it all together. You don't know what it took for that person to obtain that level of success. Just because it looked easy doesn't mean they had an easy labor. I know we want the promise to fall into our laps and miraculously appear, but you wouldn't understand the value of the promise if you didn't have to labor for it.

Let's do a quick exercise: Get a picture of an olive tree in your mind. If you don't know what an olive tree looks like, you can search for it on the internet. We'll see that the olive tree is known for durability and strength and not so easily removed.

It is mention that the olive tree can survive in all types of weather. You, my beloved, are likened to this olive tree. You are strong, courageous and mighty. Just like that tree, you are built to weather any storm you encounter in your life. There is life in the tree that sustains the olives on the branches; however, the olive is just an olive until pressure is applied to it. Once pressure is applied, it produces oil. The oil was there the whole time, but it had to go through an extraction process.

Extraction- *the action of taking out something, especially using effort or force.*

The extraction process consists of the following: Cleaning, crushing, pressing, and separation. So, which is to be valued? The process, or what was produced from the process, which is the oil. Personally, I value the oil because I know what it took for me to persevere through all of the pain, brokenness, and hard-ache. Yes, you read it correctly—not heartache, but hard-ache. As I stated before, I endured but it wasn't a teacup ride at Disney World. The hard-ache is what prompted me to fight and protect the oil that was produced in me.

For instance, if Jesus came to the world and went directly to the cross, would you see value in his life, death, and resurrection? Absolutely not! The Word of God bears witness that He persevered through tribulation, mocking, and beatings before He went to Calvary. I value Jesus' life, death, and resurrection because He went through a process and paid a price for me that I could not pay for myself.

Enduring the labor process gives us a greater appreciation that hard work is the connection to manifesting the promise. In the natural there are 3 stages of labor, which we'll view from a spiritual perspective. Every time you see the word **baby** insert the word **promise**.

Early Labor Phase: This phase is where you relax. Not lackadaisical, but you're taking your time in the process. This is the time you enjoy working on your vision boards and writing down the necessary steps you have to take in order to be skilled in your craft.

Set daily, weekly, and monthly goals. Statistics show that people who write down realistic goals have an 80% higher success rate of achieving them, versus people who don't set goals. Also take the opportunity to plan out your day and the time you'll work on your projects, which includes both your spiritual and physical growth.

Remember, we are not positioning ourselves to birth promises for material possessions or to drive the latest car. We are birthing out of relationship and covenant with the Father. The reason why God is allowing us to obtain material possessions in this season is because it's an avenue to witness and minister to God's people.

When dealing with saints, they already have a level of understanding of who the Trinity is. However, dealing with people who don't know about the Trinity, they are going to look at what you have. So, we are being positioned to look and reflect the Kingdom of God. In the early labor stage, you will feel slight cramping and contractions but nothing major, so continue to persist through the pain to prepare for the harvest.

Active Labor Phase: Normally during the last trimester, women become frustrated with being pregnant. They know the baby is due to arrive soon; however, it's not time for the baby to appear just yet. There is still some developing that must take place to bring the baby to full-term. Nonetheless, I heard some women start to do unprofitable things to induce premature labor like drinking these hocus pocus potions. (Sidebar: Naturally and spiritually stop that foolishness! My advice to you is stay the course don't speed up the process).

Whatever has been ordained for you to birth, it *will* be. Don't put yourself in a position to receive a half-promise or a partial promise. You want the promise that has been specifically handpicked for you to be birthed into its full manifestation.

Yes, you will experience growing pains at longer lengths. Yes, you will feel like you're coming out of a hailstorm heading into a tornado. Yes, the no's and the rejections will get stronger. Remember, for every "no" you receive it only takes one YES from God!

Some of the people who supported you in the beginning will turn into haters, and through all of this, the contractions are squeezing the life out of you one minute and releasing you the next. The enemy will try to get you to abort the mission and will convince you to stop building.

No matter what comes, olive tree stay active! Your activeness is shaking the kingdom of darkness. The enemy knows something is being birthed that will set the captives free and break the generational bondages of the mind of the lost and the unsaved. The scales will fall off of their eyes to see the salvation of our Lord Jesus Christ.

Active- *engaging or ready to engage in physically energetic pursuits.*

Synonyms: *progress, motion, effective, vigorous, dynamic, occupied*

Continue to pursue the promise! I love what my Pastor said, "Your condition is not your conclusion." Keep moving, keep declaring the Word of God. You are a step further in the labor process.

Transition Phase: Transparent moment: during phases one and two, I was receiving state funding assistance for food and medical care. I was unemployed and my bank account was below negative. Upon entering into the transition stage, God began to deal with me. As a result, doors to public assistance closed and all my resources dried up. I cried constantly and for a moment became weary, nevertheless I didn't stop, though I didn't understand the process.

I immediately started to pray and put God in remembrance of what He said He'd do for me, and Holy Spirit convicted me with these words: "What about the promise you made to Father? Remember when you said not my will but Thy will be done? Remember when you said be it unto me according to Thy Word? I bless and honor Holy Spirit for convicting me. It strengthened and gave me peace during the test.

I determined in my heart not to keep making promises I couldn't keep. God is the same yesterday, today and forever! His words towards us will never change and I understand now that my words towards Him should never change. Through maturity, I became higher in my thought process and I began to see the will of God for my life.

To the natural eye, the situation was detrimental, but spiritually He was teaching me how to solely depend on Him. I've learned how to survive without food, medical assistance or borrowing money. No matter how many prophecies I received about wealth and debt cancellation, the transitional phase taught me that God gives us the ability to cancel our own debt! Don't sweat this phase or get discouraged.

In the last stage, the pain intensifies, and the contractions are stronger. You may become exhausted, frustrated and impatient, but I assure you that this phase is designed to bring you into perfect alignment to receive the promise. Transition is not always easy but it is necessary.

Good news: You're almost there! Continue to breathe and speak life. Place yourself around midwives who agree with your vision and will help you deliver your baby. They will hold your hand, encourage you to keep pushing, and not to stop or give up. That will tell you to push through the weaknesses and the tiredness, so that you can receive not only the promise, but your purpose.

Special Prayer

"Father, in the name of Jesus I thank You for every reader who has taken the time to read about Your promises that will be fulfilled in their lives. I declare a newness over every mindset, every emotion, and any intellectual thoughts that would try to hinder the progress of God.

Those who are called to create businesses, I declare witty inventions, creative ideas, and I speak the spirit of a CEO in your atmosphere. I pray that everything you need from finances to buildings be provided in Jesus' name.

To those God has called into ministry, may the spirit of obedience be upon you. Go forth as an ambassador in power and demonstration. Always be apt to preach the Gospel in season and out of season. I declare that breakthrough will be in your mouth that will set the captives free. By the sound of your voice, chains will begin to fall and scales will be removed from the eyes of the unbeliever. I declare that you will be a force to be reckoned with in the earth realm.

Father, to those who are undecided, I pray that You will give revelation and understanding to the ear of the hearer. Father, You declared in

Your Word that if any of lack wisdom, let him ask of God, that giveth to all men liberally, and upbraideth not; and it shall be given him. Father, this day we move forth together in unity and declare that we were created to create! In Jesus' name, I pray. Amen."

A.R. SMITH

For more information, or to book A.R. Smith:

Email: **april@ambassadorarsmith.com**

Phone: (702) 570-2215

A R SMITH

www.ingramcontent.com/pod-product-compliance
Lightning Source LLC
Chambersburg PA
CBHW070048040426
42331CB00034B/2632